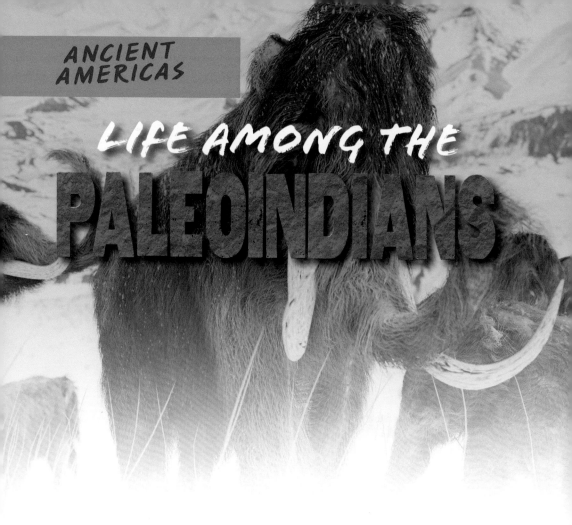

ANCIENT AMERICAS

LIFE AMONG THE

PALEOINDIANS

IAN MAHANEY

PowerKiDS
press.

NEW YORK

JUN
970.01
MAH

Published in 2017 by **The Rosen Publishing Group**
29 East 21st Street, New York, NY 10010

Developed and produced for Rosen by BlueAppleWorks Inc.

Art Director: Haley Harasymiw
Managing Editor for BlueAppleWorks: Melissa McClellan
Editor: Marcia Abramson
Design: T.J. Choleva

The illustrations in this book are based on information and sources about early humans
in general sense. Due to scarcity of information in regards to Paleoindians, they are not
necessarily historically accurate in all aspects.

Picture credits: Cover: frgrd. Buyenlarge/Shutterstock; (trees) Valentin Agapov/Shutterstock; (Clovis points)
Bill Whittaker/Wikimedia. Back cover: frgrd. Artishok/Shutterstock; bkgrd. altanaka/Shutterstock. Title page
AuntSpray/Shutterstock; p. 5 Joshua Avramson/based on image taken by Sémhur/Creative Commons;
p.10 Charles Robert Knight/Public Domain; p. 13 Daderot/Public Domain; p. 15 Joshua Avramson/based
on image taken by Wolfgang Sauber/Creative Commons; p. 17 Joshua Avramson/based on image taken by
Wolfgang Sauber/Creative Commons; p. 18 Joshua Avramson/based on image taken by Sémhur/Creative
Commons; p. 21 Joshua Avramson/based on image taken by Véronique PAGNIER/Creative Commons; p.
22 Joshua Avramson/based on image taken by Wolfgang Sauber/Creative Commons; p. 25 Museum_of_
Natural_History_Southern_Mammot/Creative Commons; p. 26 left National Park Service/Public Domain;
p. 26 Joshua Avramson/based on image taken by Ed Bierman/Creative Commons; p. 28 Joshua Avramson/
Shutterstock:Marco Prati; p. 29 Herb Roe/Creative Commons; Maps: p. 6 Joshua Avramson; p. 9 Joshua
Avramson

Cataloging-in-Publication Data
Names: Mahaney, Ian.
Title: Life among the Paleoindians / Ian Mahaney.
Description: New York : PowerKids Press, 2017. | Series: Ancient Americas | Includes index.
Identifiers: ISBN 9781508149897 (pbk.) | ISBN 9781508149835 (library bound) | ISBN 9781508149712 (6 pack)
Subjects: LCSH: Paleo-Indians--Juvenile literature. | Indians of North America--Juvenile literature.
Classification: LCC E61.M34 2017| DDC 970.01--dc23

CONTENTS

CHAPTER 1

CROSSING THE BERING STRAIT

The last ice age on Earth began between 120,000 and 60,000 years ago. It lasted until 10,000 years ago. As temperatures on Earth fell, water from the oceans froze into giant glaciers. Several times during this ice age, water moving from the oceans to glaciers caused sea levels to fall by as much as 300 feet (91 m). This drop exposed the land mass under the **Bering Strait** called Beringia. Today, the Bering Strait divides **Siberia** from Alaska, and is 55 miles (88 km) across at its narrowest point. During periods of the last ice age, the land beneath the strait formed a bridge between Russia and Alaska. Using the word "bridge" to describe Beringia underestimates the land's size. The land, Beringia, was as wide as 1,000 miles (1,600 km) across.

During periods when sea levels fell and Beringia spanned Siberia and Alaska, people and animals crossed from Asia to North America. The first animals to cross were likely a type of mammoth, Mammuthus meridionalis, or southern mammoth, about 1.8 million years ago. Sea levels rose afterwards, covering Beringia. Sea levels fell again and another **herbivore**, the musk ox, crossed Beringia 200,000 to 90,000 years ago. Musk oxen lived in herds and grew horns on their heads. When predators threatened them, musk oxen formed a circle, keeping their hindquarters together with their horns facing outwards.

HUMANS, MAMMOTHS, AND OTHER ANIMALS MIGRATED TO NORTH AMERICA DURING WHAT SCIENTISTS CALL THE PLEISTOCENE EPOCH.

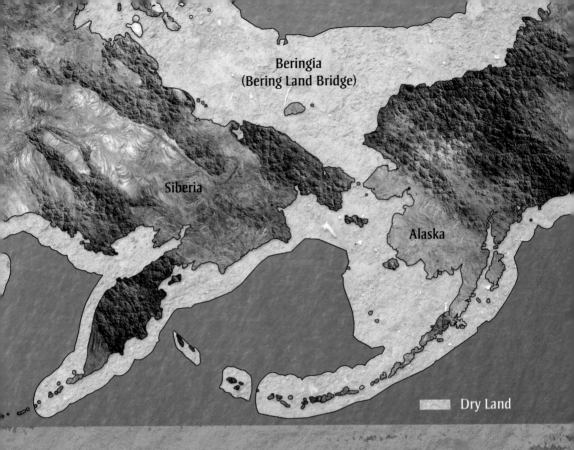

Beringia
(Bering Land Bridge)

Siberia

Alaska

Dry Land

    After musk oxen and other animals crossed Beringia, sea levels rose and fell again, and other animals made the journey across the land bridge. Another mammoth, the famous woolly mammoth, crossed Beringia at least 13,000 and maybe as many as 35,000 years ago. Though smaller than the southern mammoth, woolly mammoths were still enormous creatures. They had tusks up to 12 feet (3.7 m) long that could weigh 200 pounds (91 kg) each. Woolly mammoths could grow to 11 feet (3 m) tall at the shoulder, and weigh 12 tons (11 metric tons). By comparison, the largest land animals today, African elephants, stand 8.2 to 13 feet (2.5 to 4 m) at the shoulder, but weigh only 2.5 to 7 tons (2.3 to 6 metric tons).

Predators hunted woolly mammoths and these predators followed mammoths across Beringia. One such predator, scimitar cats, was related to saber-toothed cats. Scimitars were fast cats, faster than saber-toothed cats. Scimitars had enormous nasal openings that allowed them to swallow enormous breaths of oxygen and chase down their mammoth prey at 40 miles per hour (64 km per hour). Still these cats with canine teeth measuring four inches (10 cm) long preferred to hunt smaller mammoth calves instead of adults.

Soon after some woolly mammoths and scimitar cats left Asia, **nomadic** peoples from Siberia crossed Beringia. These people were hunters and likely followed herds of animals such as bison, mammoths, or caribou onto the land bridge. These peoples crossed the land bridge between 25,000 and 10,000 years ago.

Many historians believe all later Native American groups have their roots in these people, who have been given the name of Paleoindians. The Paleoindian period of history lasted until about 8000 B.C.

What's in the name?

The word "paleo" comes from a Greek word meaning "very old," "early," or "primitive."

CHAPTER 2

THE NEW LAND

Most scientists now agree that the first people crossed Beringia about 15,000 years ago. The evidence is buried beneath 300 feet (91 m) of water so we never may know for sure.

Many **anthropologists** think that different groups of Paleoindians walked across the land bridge at different times, but details are still being discovered. Some groups may have lived in Beringia for centuries. After reaching Alaska, they migrated along two major routes as the ice eased up in those areas. The inland route went south through the eastern Rocky Mountains, then spread out. The Pacific route went south to follow the coast, possibly using early forms of boats. It is unclear which route was used most. Either way, though, the journey was a hard one.

During the last ice age, temperatures on Earth were 2 to 18 degrees Fahrenheit (1 to 10 degrees C) colder than today. In certain places on Earth, the temperature was even colder, up to 40 degrees Fahrenheit (22 degrees C) colder than today.

In this cold world, they found many animals to hunt, but some were about to become extinct.

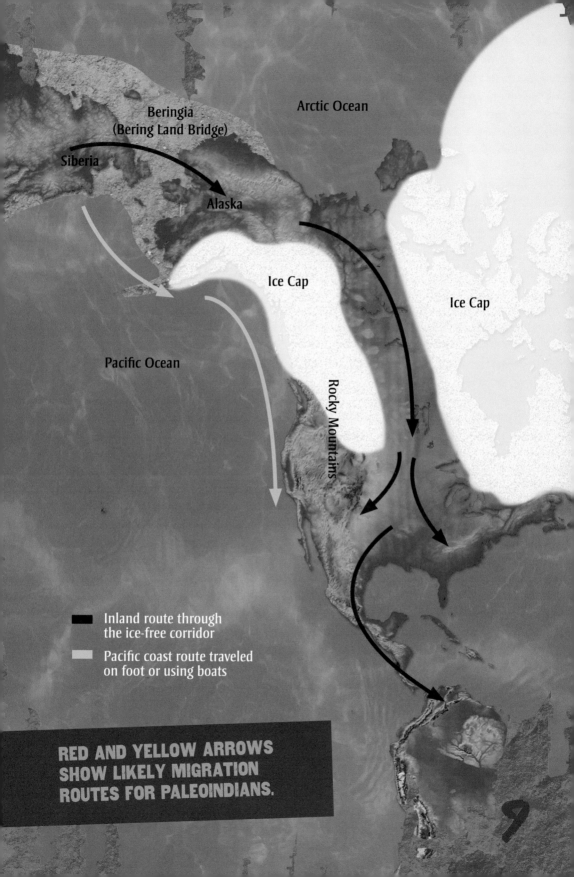

Beringia
(Bering Land Bridge)

Arctic Ocean

Siberia

Alaska

Ice Cap

Ice Cap

Pacific Ocean

Rocky Mountains

Inland route through
the ice-free corridor

Pacific coast route traveled
on foot or using boats

RED AND YELLOW ARROWS
SHOW LIKELY MIGRATION
ROUTES FOR PALEOINDIANS.

9

ANCIENT LANDSCAPE

The people on and off Beringia found a landscape filled with short grasses and shrubs, and few trees. Once the migrants began moving south into what is now Canada and the United States, they found conditions much like the **tundra** today. Similar small shrubs and grasses dominated the landscape. Temperatures kept the land cold, but the seasons were not as extreme as today. While summers were cooler than today, the great ice sheets blocked cold Arctic air from moving south in winter.

Paleoindians found **boreal** forests, the forests of evergreens and conifers common today across much of the continental United States, only once the Paleoindians reached the southernmost parts of the United States.

THE NOMADS FOUND NEW PREY IN NORTH AMERICA, INCLUDING HERDS OF NATIVE MASTODON, A DISTANT COUSIN OF THE MAMMOTH.

LIVING IN BERINGIA

A recent scientific theory suggests that humans stayed in Beringia for up to 10,000 years before moving out across the Americas. Fossil samples show that Beringia's tundra had oasis-like spots where shrubs, trees, and grasses grew. Animals could have lived there, and people would have found prey to hunt, fuel for fires, and material to make shelters in Beringia. Some scientists now think the nomads may have been stuck in Beringia because giant ice sheets and glaciers blocked their way into Alaska and even back to Asia. When the ice began to melt, and as water rose over Beringia again, the migration continued.

The inhabited places on Beringia would be underwater for centuries by now, but scientists are trying to find them with new technologies. If they do, much more may be discovered about these early human travelers.

ANCIENT ANIMALS

Herbivores such as bison, elk, bighorn sheep, Pleistocene horses, mastodons, and mammoths ate the grasses. Mastodons were new prey for the nomads, as these animals lived only in North and Central America. They looked like mammoths but were a bit smaller. People also found predators ready to prey on the herbivores. Scimitar cats were already extinct, but the migrants found lions and bears. Short-faced bears were as tall as a person when the bear stood on all four legs. These bears weighed up to 2,500 pounds (1,100 kg). The migrants saw American lions that weighed 500 pounds (230 kg), bigger than lions in Africa today. Smaller animals, from squirrels to deer, were also plentiful.

CHAPTER 3

ANCIENT CLOVIS PEOPLE

Paleoindians shared many features with their Asian ancestors. For example, both peoples were hunter-gatherers, built fires, and domesticated dogs. In about 1930, **archaeologists** found evidence that Paleoindians began to **diverge** from their Asian ancestors soon after they arrived on the new continent. Spear tips were found near Clovis, New Mexico, that gave a name to a whole group of Paleoindian cultures. These grooved spear tips are called Clovis points and their makers are called Clovis people. The Clovis people used the grooves to attach poles to their carved spear points. Ranging from 1 inch (2.5 cm) long to 5 inches (12.5 cm) long, Clovis points have been found among the bones of mammoths and bison, showing that these early Americans hunted large animals, the megafauna.

The Clovis people hunted large megafauna, but they searched for smaller mammals and birds, too. They fished with spears. They **foraged** for plants. The Clovis people were early hunter-gatherers and they spread across the modern day continental United States. They also lived in southern Canada and Mexico.

PEOPLE STILL FIND CLOVIS POINTS IN THE GROUND TODAY, AND EXCELLENT EXAMPLES CAN BE SEEN IN MUSEUMS ALL OVER THE AMERICAS.

13

The Clovis people lived and spread out across the United States beginning between 11,000 and 13,000 years ago. They lived until 11,000 to 9,000 years ago when their groups and descendants turned less nomadic, and into more distinctive and settled Native American groups.

The Clovis people or their ancestors followed the land bridge across Beringia into Alaska. The glacier that covered most of Canada began melting soon afterwards. By approximately 12,000 years ago, the glacier had sufficiently melted and formed a corridor in western Canada. One glacier split into two glaciers, and anthropologists think the Clovis people or their ancestors followed the corridor between the glaciers. Another likely route took some of the earliest Americans down the Pacific coast on foot or by early forms of boat.

SPREADING OUT

The Clovis people spread quickly across the continental United States. Archaeologists have found evidence of Clovis people in every state except Alaska and Hawaii.

Who was in Chile?

Scientists have found that humans were living at a site in Chile. This has begun a debate about whether some early groups came to the Americas by sea.

THE ATLATL APPEARED EARLY IN PALEOINDIAN CULTURE AND ITS USE WAS STILL WIDESPREAD AT THE TIME OF THE FIRST EUROPEAN CONTACT.

The biggest Clovis site is in Gault, Texas. Archaeologists have found more than half of Clovis era **artifacts** at this site, also known as the Buttermilk Creek site. They've found Clovis points, engraved bones, and spear throwers called atlatls. An atlatl is a stick that helped Clovis people throw a spear further.

The Gault site is an interesting archaeology dig site. For many years, archaeologists thought the Clovis people were the first inhabitants of North America. As they dug in the Gault site and discovered Clovis artifacts, they also found evidence that people lived in North America longer than the Clovis people. That proved that Clovis people were not the first people to inhabit the continent, although they were one of the most important. Clovis culture disappeared for reasons that remain unclear, but the Clovis people do link to the cultures that next evolved.

15

CHAPTER 4

LIFE IN THE VASTNESS OF THE NEW CONTINENT

Paleoindians found a range of animals, or **fauna**, across the Americas. They also found a variety of **flora**, plant life. This range helps explain the ways Paleoindians found food. The Paleoindians were hunter-gatherers. These people walked the land seeking animals to hunt or fish, and plants such as berries, nuts, seeds, and roots to gather. They were small groups of nomadic peoples who didn't settle in one area, but followed herds or animals, hunting and searching for food.

Anthropologists believe they have a good idea of how Paleoindians lived, based on studies of later foraging cultures. Small groups lived in a vast area, and they could go for months without seeing other humans. This also meant that groups did not have to compete for food, so when they did meet, relations were friendly. Meetings likely turned into celebrations, and some were arranged in advance. Often there was a wedding, as these meetings were an opportunity to make marriages outside of family groups.

Over time the Paleoindians spread out through the Americas. Regional cultures began to develop, but they all made and used similar stone tools. More changes came later as they began to farm and live in permanent settlements.

PALEOINDIAN GROUPS HUNTED AND GATHERED OVER WIDE AREAS TO FIND ENOUGH FOOD FOR THEIR BANDS.

FAMILY STRUCTURE

Paleoindian families spent large amounts of time in small family groups that archaeologists call bands. A family may have only included a man, woman, and children. A larger family group may have included grandparents, aunts, and uncles. Families often worked with other families when they needed to hunt, though. They worked together in groups of 20 to 50 people.

Like many societies, Paleoindians split duties among men and women. Groups of men hunted while women cared for the household and children. Women also softened animal hides with stone tools so the Paleoindians could use the hides for tents and clothing.

The Paleoindians moved every few days, so they had to travel light, with few possessions. They built simple, temporary shelters or stayed in caves.

MOTHERS CARED FOR YOUNG CHILDREN AT THE GROUP'S MAIN CAMP DURING HUNTS. THOSE TOO OLD TO HUNT HELPED THEM.

THE END OF THE MEGAFAUNA

The first nomads to cross the land bridge found and hunted a kind of animal that was about to become extinct. Scientists have named these animals "megafauna," which means "very large animal," and especially those that lived during the last ice age. Mammoths and mastodons, which were distant relatives of today's elephants, towered over the ice age landscape. There were also dire wolves that looked like giant hyenas and saber-toothed cats with jaws like a shark's. More familiar animals existed in giant forms, too. An average beaver today might weigh about 45 pounds (20 kg). Now imagine one that weighs 300 pounds (136 kg)! There were also super-sized versions of ground sloths, tapirs, horses, tortoises, reindeer, armadillos, oxen, moose, capybaras, and other animals.

This feast of giant prey did not last long for the Paleoindians. Soon after the humans arrived, the megafauna species disappeared. The glaciers were melting, and the environment that supported the megafauna was vanishing. Humans were able to adapt, but the megafauna could not. Their diets, habitats, and reproductive cycles were linked to their ice age environment. Some scientists think that hunting by the Paleoindians may have hastened the extinctions, but others do not agree. They point out that similar extinctions had happened before there were any humans around.

HUNTING METHODS

Meat was a key part of the Paleoindian diet. They could not be certain of how well plants were growing, but they could track animals. At first they used spears to hunt megafauna such as mammoth and a now-extinct kind of bison. Men hunted big and small animals, but it is likely that older children and women hunted for small animals, too.

Plenty of food was available during the brief warm season, but the Paleoindians also knew how and where to hunt during the long winter.

When Paleoindian men hunted together, they used the size of their group as a weapon against their prey much as they used spears or atlatls to hunt. Whether hunting in groups or alone, Paleoindians often stalked prey by water. When the prey came to drink, the Paleoindians pounced with their spears or other tools. Hunters also worked in groups to trap animals or scare them off cliffs. If a group of Paleoindians hunted bison and scared the animals off a cliff, they had an easier time killing injured prey after the prey fell. Just as they adjusted to the weather, the Paleoindians hunted smaller prey animals as the megafauna became extinct.

FOOD GATHERING

Paleoindian women also gathered food for the family. They asked their children to help, and taught the boys and girls to collect vegetables and berries, roots, seeds, and bulbs. They even made small meals combining berries with meat. They needed lightweight containers for food, so they wove baskets or made them from bark or leather. When gathering food, Paleoindians often brought domesticated dogs along for the journey. Outfitted with a **travois** or sled, the Paleoindians attached the travois to the dog with a harness and the dog pulled the sled full of food home.

DWELLINGS AND CLOTHING

Paleoindians spread across the Americas, and they adapted to their surroundings and resources they found. They wore clothing made from plant fibers and furs or hides of animals they hunted.

Paleoindians moved depending on their needs. They often made tools for hunting in one location. They even stayed there repeatedly. They lived in wood structures covered with bark or animal skins while they made these tools. They then moved to temporary housing to hunt. They often camped near water, and stayed in caves or a kind of tent that could be put up quickly. Shelters were made from animal skins, wood, and brush. Some looked like a short tepee.

PALEOINDIANS BUILT SIMPLE HUNTING CAMPS FROM WHATEVER NATURAL MATERIALS WERE AVAILABLE.

WHEN THEY WERE NEAR FRESH WATER OR THE OCEAN, PALEOINDIANS WOULD CATCH OR SPEAR FISH AND GATHER SHELLFISH TO EAT.

ANNUAL MIGRATIONS

Similar to moving based on their activity, Paleoindians also moved based on the seasons. They followed their prey. When bison herds or other prey moved hundreds of miles (or kilometers) south in the winter to find abundant food, Paleoindians trailed the animals. For example, Paleoindians from Pennsylvania to Alabama followed seasonal paths as they hunted large mammals like bison or caribou. Depending on the area of North America, Paleoindians followed smaller game, too. Some even followed fish **spawning** routes.

CONTACT AND TRADE

Groups of Paleoindians did not live in **isolation**. They interacted with other groups of hunter-gatherers. Archaeologists know this because they've discovered groups of Paleoindians who possessed tools made far from the groups' hunting grounds and bases for tool making. However, they left behind few physical clues about other details of their daily life. Their religious practices, language, customs, and celebrations were lost over time.

Paleoindians needed high-quality stones for their hunting blades and other tools. If proper stones were not available in their particular location, they traded with other groups to get them. Archaeologists have found stones in Pennsylvania that Paleoindians could only have found in New York. They have found fish hooks in Alabama that trading partners made in the Arctic. What's more, archaeologists more often found these foreign tools and stones at Paleoindian bases for tool making than their temporary hunting grounds. This means that Paleoindian groups trading with one another knew where they could find their trading partners.

Tools of the trade

Paleoindians excelled at making tools out of stone, which helped them survive. They created specialized tools for scraping hides, cutting meat, punching holes, and other tasks.

23

CHAPTER 5

DOCUMENTING THE PAST

Archaeologists have a tough yet exciting job using artifacts to construct the history of people. Since archaeologists cannot return to the time people walked from Siberia to North America, they use clues in artifacts they find.

Archaeologists have found similar hunter-gatherer tools on both sides of Beringia. In Diuktai Cave in northeast Siberia, archaeologists found stone tools, spears, and knives called microblades. Archaeologists found very similar microblades more than 1,000 miles (1,600 km) away at a site near Fairbanks in central Alaska. This helped archaeologists link people on two continents.

Important clues also have come from sites where mammoth and mastodon bones have been found with Clovis points and artifacts. Archaeologists are learning about how and where Paleoindians lived from studying sites such as Mastodon State Park in Missouri.

Based on these studies, a time line has been set for the history of Native Americans. The Paleoindians were followed by the **Archaic** period, which lasted from about 8000 to 1000 B.C., and the Woodland period from 1000 B.C. to as late as A.D. 1600.

MUSEUMS ALL OVER THE WORLD DISPLAY SKELETONS OF MAMMOTHS AND MASTODONS, INCLUDING THIS SOUTHERN MAMMOTH IN PARIS, FRANCE.

25

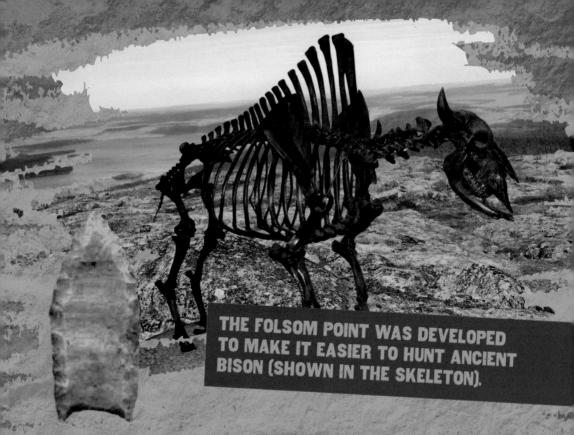

THE FOLSOM POINT WAS DEVELOPED TO MAKE IT EASIER TO HUNT ANCIENT BISON (SHOWN IN THE SKELETON).

THE FOLSOM PEOPLE

Archaeologists found important tools called Folsom points before other archaeologists found Clovis points. Without any knowledge of Clovis points, archaeologists felt the Folsom people were the first Paleoindians. They later learned the Clovis people **predated** Folsom people because Folsom points were an improved version of Clovis points. Bison were smaller and faster than the now extinct mammoths and mastodons, so hunters needed to strike quickly with sharper, smaller spear tips. Archaeologists also learned that while Clovis people spread across the continent, Folsom people lived on the western plains of the United States where they hunted the big mammals.

FINDING THE BISON HUNTERS

Archaeologists discovered the Folsom culture at a site in Folsom, New Mexico. According to local legend, the Folsom site first was found by an African American cowboy in 1908. Excavations began in the 1920s. Folsom points and other stone tools were discovered at the site along with bones from large extinct bison, especially a species called Bison antiquus. By using modern technology, scientists have dated the site to between 9000 B.C. and 8000 B.C. That was when the Folsom people developed their specialized culture based on bison hunting. Anthropologists believe the Folsom people learned to hunt cooperatively by surrounding the bison and killing as many as 50 in one hunt. This required planning and teamwork, skills that helped the Folsom people survive. Today the Folsom site is a National Historic Landmark.

ARCHAIC CULTURES

Using artifacts, archaeologists found that Native Americans began living in more permanent housing after the Paleoindians. Archaic cultures are collections of Native Americans who began living in more permanent shelters. Archaic cultures also began using tools made of bone and growing plants. Archaic cultures started the agricultural traditions of Native Americans. They domesticated corn, **amaranth**, and squash, among other plants, and set the path for further Native American cultures.

Through a record of artifacts, archaeologists learned that Archaic Native Americans were the transition between the hunting and gathering, nomadic Paleoindians and groups of Native Americans who lived in more permanent settlements.

27

ARCHAIC CULTURES STILL HUNTED WITH SPEARS. BOWS AND ARROWS WERE DEVELOPED IN THE LATE WOODLAND PERIOD AROUND A.D. 500.

Though they might still follow animals on seasonal migrations, the Native Americans lived in the same homes year after year.

EASTERN WOODLAND CULTURE

Archaic groups lived from the end of the Paleoindian period until 4,000 years ago when Eastern Woodland and other cultures began developing into unique traditions though they often followed some of the same customs. Many Woodland Native Americans lived in villages along streams or rivers. They still hunted by these rivers, but planted corn and squash, and lived in permanent wigwams or longhouses. Many of these tribes also built burial mounds. One such group, the Hopewell Culture,

NORTH AMERICAN MOUND BUILDERS

Native groups from the Great Lakes to the Gulf of Mexico and from the Mississippi River eastward built great earthen mounds in many different shapes and sizes. Some were burial mounds and others were used for religious ceremonies. This Mound Builder culture lasted from about 3500 B.C. to the late 1500s. Anthropologists believe the culture disappeared because so many of its people died from diseases carried by Europeans.

was based in Ohio with related groups stretching from Kansas to New York. These mounds were burial chambers that ranged from 50 to 100 feet (15 to 30 m) in diameter. Eastern Woodland Indians passed these developments and agriculture on to other Native American traditions.

The Woodland period often is said to have ended in A.D. 1000, but the culture actually continued in some areas until the arrival of Europeans. In the northeast United States, for example, the Iroquois and other groups kept their way of life into the late 1500s.

SPANISH EXPLORERS WROTE DETAILED ACCOUNTS OF MOUND BUILDER CITIES THEY VISITED. THIS DRAWING RE-CREATES A SITE IN ILLINOIS BASED ON SUCH ACCOUNTS.

GLOSSARY

amaranth: a plant with flowers that people grow for food. The seeds are used like a grain.

anthropologists: scientists who study the history and society of humans

archaeologists: scientists who study the remains of peoples from the past to understand how they lived

archaic: relating to past or ancient times

artifacts: objects created and produced by humans that help archaeologists study the past

Bering Strait: the narrow passage of water (strait) that connects the Bering Sea with the Arctic Ocean

boreal: part of or related to northern regions, especially forests

diverge: to split or become different

fauna: the animal life of a region

flora: the plant life of a region

foraged: hunted or searched for something

herbivore: an animal that eats plants

isolation: the state of being alone, away from others

nomadic: roaming about from place to place

predated: existed or happened at an earlier time

Siberia: an area farthest north and east in Russia

spawning: laying eggs in water

travois: a platform Native Americans attached to a dog or horse for carrying supplies

tundra: a cold, treeless area with permanently frozen soil

FOR MORE INFORMATION

BOOKS

Doak, Robin S. *Arctic Peoples*. Chicago: Heinemann-Raintree Library, 2011.

Kunz, Michael L. *The Mesa Site: Paleoindians Above the Arctic Circle*. Seattle: Amazon CreateSpace, 2015.

Murphree, Daniel S. *Native America: A State-by-state Historical Encyclopedia*. Santa Barbara, CA: ABC-CLIO, 2012.

WEBSITES

Due to the changing nature of Internet links, PowerKids Press has developed an online list of websites related to the subject of this book. This site is updated regularly. Please use this link to access the list:

www.powerkidslinks.com/aa/paleo

INDEX